Stay For Lunch

For information, contact:

Pleasurable Pause Press, LLC

1730 White Ave., Beloit, WI 53511

www.pleasurablepausepress.com

FIRST EDITION

Designed by Jeff Larson, The Larson Group

Printed by Signature Book Printing, www.sbpbooks.com

Library of Congress Cataloging-in-Publication Data is available upon request.

ISBN 978-0-9816499-0-0

This is for Matthew, Rob and Ben.

And of course, Francina.

Mrs. Anne Goodwin
___ White Ave.

Anne, dear — I loved
our visit only it was
too short. The Nicks (?)
tea was special, thank
you so much. I
enjoyed it so much —
you look wonderful —
I hate for you to live
so far away, but it
does look as if it
was a good move
for you. I do hope
the new business
is working out fine
and we must remember
that a venture of that
size takes a while
to build. I'm glad
that Matthew has a
group to perform with
and really "cal" it takes
him to church.
I wish I could see
your two boys. I
know you are

Stay For Lunch

A Story of Faith and Friendship

Anne Goodwin

Francina.

A name, a person, an angel on earth.

A dear, dear friend.

My story about my friendship with Francina can begin at the beginning; because there was a specific moment our friendship began. There was life before Francina and life after Francina...

I will always remember my first glimpse of her. It happened during a pensive morning drive, through an old Atlanta neighborhood while my head was full of endings in my life—the recent death of my grandmother, an unplanned pregnancy ending in miscarriage – I literally forced myself out of bed to try to make it to my office by 10:00 a.m.

As I lethargically followed the curve around the Ansley Country Club, I watched as if in slow motion, an accident occur. Two cars collided. The three cars ahead of me ignored the plight blocking most of the road and drove on by.

Somewhere in my self-pitying haze I heard the voice of Mr. Swanson, Mr. Drivers Ed, speak, "If you witness an accident you must stop, you must render aid." I stopped my car and hesitantly approached the car that had been broadsided.

A whisper of a figure bent over the wheel. I opened the door and was greeted by a tiny, lovely, snow-white haired woman. She smiled at me as if I had just arrived for tea and busily reached for a yellow legal pad next to her seat.

It was then that I noticed the bone sticking out of her left shin. "My name is Francina K., and I wonder if you could do something for me," she responded, as I asked her what hospital she would prefer the ambulance to come from and whether I could notify family for her.

"The first thing you must do for me is this." She handed me the yellow notepad with her instructions. I rushed into the house of a concerned woman who had joined the scene. As I looked down at the pad, I called someone named Viola and found myself saying, "Francina will not be able to make *bridge* this morning, she is terribly sorry but she has had a slight accident."

Francina and I held hands the first four hours of our friendship. Her son and daughter-in-law were not to be found and after a frustrating conversation with a vague housekeeper about a tennis club somewhere in greater Atlanta, I returned to Francina and grabbed her hand. We didn't let go for a long time. As we waited in the emergency room, Francina sighed and squeezed, "I'm so disappointed. I'm afraid that this will change everything and I've been doing so well."

I learned that this eighty-six year old woman, who recently moved from the tiny town of Griffin, Georgia to be closer to family, had purchased a condo in a golf community (just minutes away from my office I discovered) in the middle of Atlanta, and loved it.

Sort of Mary Tyler Moore all grown up.

Her composure and strength floored me. The only sign of her physical discomfort came in a few beads of perspiration on the top of her lip and the growing paleness of her skin against her white hair and cream colored dickey, which she chose to keep on.

Although she fretted about "ruining everything" she also paid attention to me and drew out my melancholy. I don't remember all that we shared but it was intimate and genuine, as was every conversation I've since had with Francina.

A mutual trust formed immediately. As the hours passed in typical Emergency Room slow motion we awaited news from Francina's family (I distinctly remember hoping it was a good one who appreciated the jewel they had in Francina).

After moving for a third time to a different emergency room cubicle, my tending to Francina was interrupted by a concerned, thoroughly Southern female voice exclaiming, "Namawwww, what on earth happened, are you alright?", and a burst of post-tennis energy entered the room in the form of Nancy, Francina's daughter-in-law. I was so relieved to discover that Francina was someone's cherished Namaw. I dropped her hand, moved to the side and said my farewell. Did I mention that Francina and I discovered that we were reading the same novel?

I left the hospital, my head full of Francina, and my heart inexplicably lighter than it had been in a long time.

"Anne dear, please help yourself to another sandwich." My eyes coveted the platter of Francina's crustless delicacies.

The moment I walked into her home, I felt embraced by nostalgia and familiar things. I could have been visiting Nanny, my own grandmother with her lifetime collection of lovely pieces, colors and photographs of a large, playful family poised in every spare space.

Francina called and invited me to her house when she returned home from her hospital stay; we had communicated by notes and phone during her confinement after surgery. "I have something I must give you for being such an angel to me, please come for lunch."

She presented me with a white butcher-paper wrapped present and declared she didn't know what the "*propah* present would be to thank me for what I had done." So she decided on a beef tenderloin.

We both laughed.

That day began a wonderful biweekly ritual of shared lunches and errand running with Francina. We first would sit in her sun-room and chat about everything.

I learned of her life shared with her husband Wib, who unfortunately died at the age of fifty-eight but left her feeling rich in love. I paged through sepia drenched photographs of a beautiful young woman with a tall handsome man water-skiing side by side, hunting in gaiters together and raising a family throughout the South's small textile towns.

I read stories of Francina's excursions as a Girl Scout leader–she took the first group of girls to Norway to camp on the fjords–and listened to her accompanying tales of travel through Europe in the days when travel was an art and an adventure.

(Francina came by her spirit for exploration naturally-her mother in the early 1900's yearned to travel the country by train, so she reserved her own Pullman car and started Mrs. Cook's Travel Tours. Francina recalled being hooked up and released from trains all across America.)

Our errands were full of good fun. We scooted from dry cleaners to grocers to banks and then the liquor store, all the way following Francina's path of right turns only, since left turns are notorious trouble in curvy, hilly Atlanta. It was a left hand turn that was Francina's undoing at the Ansley Country Club.

All this in my red Honda civic two door.

Francina lived in the moment and was intent on staying "current". She mentioned to me one afternoon as we drove that she would appreciate me keeping her on track and requested, "Please Anne, if I start repeating myself, just say, 'Francina, I enjoyed that story so much the *first* time you told me' and I'll move on." She certainly kept current on my life. Although I relished the stories she shared with me, she was much more interested in my challenges and struggles both professionally and personally.

I was fortunate to go through my first successful pregnancy with Francina. Sitting in her antique-filled dining room, with my appetite that was beyond polite, she would always expect me to eat everything laid out on the table as she daintily nibbled on half of a sandwich. To this day I wonder if she was politely starving herself, unsure of what I would unabashedly consume.

Francina came to a baby shower, held for me after the baby was born, since my son, Robby, chose to appear three weeks ahead of schedule.

I was a new, nervous, nursing mom and wasn't quite sure what was expected of me when the guest of honor demanded his next meal. My host's sixty-something 'old school' mother escorted me back to the bedroom where I could nurse privately. I sat there missing my own party as this well-intended relative stranger stood sentry outside the bedroom door.

I was so relieved to hear Francina's steady footsteps coming down the hall. Gently but firmly she pushed past the aghast guard and sat down on the side of the bed with me, saying, "Anne dear, I do so want a chance to visit before I leave. How are you doing, sweetie?"

And one by one my friends all came and joined me as the little guy happily suckled. Thanks to Francina I never blinked about nursing again.

Francina lived life large in faith. She radiated faith and sprinkled some to share each step along the way. I've been the happy recipient of those sprinkles often. Actually, I credit my determination to enjoy life based on faith as opposed to fear solely on my relationship with Francina.

I remember when we first broached the topic of faith and God and living. It was probably during that first lunch we shared in her house. I was a skeptical Episcopalian who was married to a recovering Catholic; our spirituality existed basically untapped. Organized churches held little allure.

At the time I met Francina, I recognized a void that marked the beginning of my spiritual journey that continues today.

Francina has been my beacon.

We discussed destiny and prayer one day. Francina described a powerful moment in her life where she sought spiritual guidance: she was torn as she had simultaneously been asked to be a member of the National Girl Scout Board which would require much travel and time spent in New York City (a big carrot to dangle in front of a Griffin, Georgia gal) and to be a team leader in her church for young adolescents which would require much time at home involved in church activities. Mutually exclusive honors on which she walked the fence.

She said "I prayed to the Lord real hard day and night asking him to show me the way to the right decision. And as I prayed and prayed I heard a voice very strongly say inside me, 'Don't do either.' Well I was flabbergasted. That was not the answer I was looking for but I went ahead and declined them both. Three months later my husband died, totally unexpectedly, and I would have been unable to fulfill either obligation".

Crisis hit my life soon after that conversation, and prayer entered my life as well. We received the phone call at 2:00 am that all parents dread. Our sixteen year-old son (my husband's son from his first marriage whom I love as my own) suffered a head injury in a car accident and was not expected to make it through the night. We traveled through that long night home to Wisconsin to find Tom in a coma barely hanging on.

One of the first people I called in the wee hours of the morning, back in Atlanta, was Francina. She gave me a lifeline to hold onto throughout that day and the weeks and months of coma to follow.

Her message was simple, "Anne, there will be people who tell you and Matthew that this is God's will for Tom. I don't believe that. God does not intend for Tom to be suffering from this accident. But God gave man free will and in that free will accidents happen. It's God's *love* that will wrap around you and give you and your family the strength to help Tom through this. "

I've carried that message inside my heart for years now and know that when life becomes tricky, as it often does, I can rely on the faith Francina helped set free inside me. Maybe it wasn't Mr. Drivers Ed's voice I heard that day after all.

Love

"Anne, dear, it's so wonderful to have you here. I must admit something very strange is happening with me. I think I might be experiencing a slight *depression*. Have you ever heard of anything so silly? I just don't understand it."

"Francina," I replied as I sat back in the dining room chair, instantly putting aside thoughts of getting back to the office any time soon, "you have pneumonia. Of course you are depressed. You deserve to be. Pneumonia is tough to beat and it takes a long time to get back to 100 percent."

"Do you *really* think so sweetie? I have felt so unlike

myself". "As you should, you are sick," I said. "You

need to give yourself a break. It's OK to feel blue."

Of course what stunned me was that even though the

puff had been taken out of Francina's sail, she sat at

the head of her dining room table looking perfectly

lovely, as always. She pondered what I had said briefly

and then began to sparkle a tiny bit as she remarked,

"I guess you're right. I feel better *already* just knowing

that I'm *supposed* to feel bad. Thank you." It was

at that moment I realized Francina looked to our

friendship for support and guidance as much as I did.

Fifty-odd years between us and we were girlfriends,

helping each other along our respective paths.

Our paths came to a crossroad after almost three years of cozy lunches, cherished chats and special events. One year Francina attended our annual Dance Hall Jam, a music evening we hosted in an old rustic camp cabin at our 1940's Atlanta Pool Club.

My husband Matthew's gifted songwriting, guitar playing and performing talents have blessed us with many musical friends. We celebrated those friendships annually with an unpredictable evening of acoustic performances. I was delighted the year Francina responded "yes" to our invitation and arrived at what turned out to be the first "jam" of her life.

Accompanied by her ascotted son and spirited daughter-in-law, she sat in her lawn chair with her portable beverage of choice, surrounded by an assortment of cheese, pâté and crackers as if she were in the middle of Chastain Park waiting for the Atlanta Symphony to begin.

After appreciating the uniqueness of "Matt the Congo Man" and some earnest folk troubadours, Francina heard Matthew perform for the first time. He dedicated a heart-wrenching love song wrought from the time our relationship was tested by long distance (which basically beckoned me to Atlanta) titled, "Follow My Tears" to Francina.

A quiet remained over the Dance Hall as Matthew finished the song and then Francina's voice rose from the back of the room. "Matthew honey, would it be *propah* for me to say something here? *Nevah* in my life have I *evah* experienced such a thing as tonight's party. I thank you for that beautiful song and I am so glad that it had a happy ending because if it hadn't, then I would never have met Anne and all of you and that would have been a *disastah*."

Later I discovered Francina had attended our Dance Hall Jam with two crushed vertebrae from falling earlier that day.

FOLLOW MY TEARS
Lyrics and music by Matthew Goodwin

if you wanted to know what i'm seeing as our love seems to slip
out of sight then baby follow my tears 'cross the lines of my face
in the dark as i lay here at night...baby follow my tears
   we've been lovers so long, we're so strong
   we always take the trouble to find out we've never been wrong
   and we're the kind of lovers everybody ought to be
   we always talk things over, make it so easy to see
   and we've been loving so strong for so long
   its been so easy to find out we've never been wrong
   why take chances, why give in to the fears?
   when we can hide behind this happiness for years
if you wanted to know what i'm seeing as our love seems to slip
out of sight then baby follow my tears 'cross the lines of my face
in the dark as i lay here at night...baby follow my tears
   we've been lucky so far but we're pushing the odds
   and if we wait too long we could lose everything that we've got
   we've got to find the courage we need to make up our minds
   we've got to come together before we run out of time
so if you wanted to know what i'm seeing as our love seems to slip
out of sight then baby follow my tears 'cross the lines of my face
in the dark as i lay here at night
and if you wanted to know what i'm feeling about this distance
that keeps us apart then baby follow my tears as they run down
my face
   into this ocean that is drowning my heart, baby follow my tears

Ann, dear — I'm back home
and plan to stay a while. In
early June I go to the —
to the Bear — a happy time —
and it was so good to have
that little ___ with you
afterwards ___ ___ we went
to Arizona ___

and I told you all this.
Do forgive — Margaret & John Horton have
a darling place in the mts. &
they plan to take me up there
for a visit soon and I'm
looking forward. They will play
tennis & I will read ___
a couple ___

I'm ___
and ___
again ___

Anne, dear — I loved
___ visit, only it was ___
___ it. The Nicks (?)
___ special, thank
___ much — I
___ much.
___ beautiful —
___ you to the
___ but it
___ if it
___ have
___ hope
___ fine
___ ___
___ will
___ a
___ with
___ ___
___ take
___ see

Poppies
J. J. Walther (1600–1679)
Watercolour
The Victoria & Albert Museum, London

a ___ treated. I go
back to him tomorrow.
He froze it and it's
(benign) ___ about well. I'm still
trying to get organized —
but the ___. I feel
at home. This place is a
community within it-
self. I'm involved in
the Stephen ministry — an
effort to be 'a friend' to
someone in some sort of
crisis. Do this with the
guidance of the Pavillion
(infirmary) administrator.
There's much more to it than
that.
We had a pipe break recently
and flooded the ground floor —
all the floor covering ruined.
It's been good to chat with
you — I love
you —
Fondly, Fran

The next month I found myself sitting in Francina's sun room while she recuperated telling her that there would be no more annual Dance Hall Jams in Atlanta. Matthew, Robby and I were moving back to Wisconsin. Our chats turned into notes, our friendship grew through thoughts on paper. We both faced change.

Our move to a small community in southern Wisconsin and Francina's decision to relocate to a very elegant Peachtree Road retirement community (choosing, of course, a top floor apartment with a spectacular view of Atlanta bursting below her) offered us much to contemplate together. We advised and empathized when describing our adjustments.

Francina struggled with planned community living. She much preferred to discuss the Crisis Management Training course she participated in "off-site" rather than the efforts of trying to get a "fourth" together for Wednesday's lunch in the hotel-like dining room.

I prepared for the birth of my second son amongst strangers longing for the comfort that surrounded me in Georgia. Unfortunately, I was drugged and assaulted during the delivery of my son by a temporary, traveling on-call doctor and found myself in a huge emotional and physical tailspin after Ben's birth.

With time and healing, Francina's gentle counsel helped guide me to a decision of action, which is how I found myself at our local Police Department reporting the crime in what seemed to be an interrogation room; my two-month old son gurgling at the single bright light in the ceiling.

I believed in frequent visits to Atlanta, with Francina always my first stop. Her apartment, although smaller than her condominium, retained the essence of Francina's rich life.

Even though the larger pieces of furniture were gone, the familiar memorabilia remained and surrounded us cozily. I found her bedroom, custom painted in Francina's trademark pink, very reassuring.

Our visits often included my friend, Jeanne. We liked to take Francina to Tea at one of the Peachtree Road hotels. One early spring we pulled into the pink azalea-lined drive and found Francina waiting at the front door dressed in a plaid suit the colors of a deep, rich Easter basket.

Something didn't seem quite right though and it wasn't until we had settled into our corner in the light filled Hotel Nikko, champagne glasses in hand, tea sandwiches present, that Francina chose to fill us in.

"Girls, I have a *dilemma*. We all *love* the little girl who does our hair at Canterbury Court" (her community has a resident hair dresser) "and we really do find her to be just *precious*, but we all *hate* our hair!"

That was it. I looked at Francina and realized her lovely head of white had become a mixture of pastels all seemingly growing on various geometric planes. Francina was askew.

Fortunately, Jeanne promised to come with a portable Lady Remington hair dryer (one she had recently acquired at a favorite "treasures" antique market) to secretly reclaim Francina in the privacy of her own apartment.

As we finished our visit that afternoon, Francina sat back, pleased with our plan, looked up at the Japanese waterfall and pronounced, "This room just *carries* me away".

That's my last bright image of Francina. The next
visit came preceded by tidal waves of emotion. An
impulsive, overdue call on the telephone to Francina
brought an unfamiliar male voice to my ear. "Allo?"
Hang up and try again. "Allo, you have reached a
vacant apartment, who are you trying to reach?" Panic
and chill set in stone as I called the switchboard for
news about Francina's whereabouts.

Had her family not thought to call me with the news
of her passing? Is our friendship only ours? Do I not
count? Is Francina gone? Relief freed me as I waited for
the operator to direct my call to the Infirmary/Assisted
Living area of her community. Francina had a new
telephone number and a new life.

During my regular June trip to Atlanta, I braced
myself as I approached our first visit together after her
admittance to the infirmary.

"Sweetie, it's something to do with my heart. It's not like it's having *attacks* or anything, it's just not right". She reassuredly grabbed my hand as I peered anxiously in front of her. I looked past the Francina leaning fraily against a restraining pad in a wheelchair, and found her sweet eyes looking right into mine. "Now, tell me, what's new with Matthew and the boys?". Our visit was brief and as I left Francina, I gave her a copy of the first draft of my notes on our friendship.

"Anne, dear, I'm afraid that you've been too generous."

"No, Francina, I am writing straight from my heart."

"Well then, that's your heart speaking directly to mine. I can't begin to tell you what this means to me; you know that what we share is very special."

We sat holding each others' hand. She continued, "Would you mind if I shared this with my family? We have a reunion in the North Georgia mountains which I hope I'll be well enough to attend." "Francina, please do. I would be honored," I replied.

Later that visit, Francina amazed me one more time. She asked about Tom, our twenty-three year old who's faced life with unique challenges since his head injury when he was sixteen.

I explained that he was well, studying Geography in college and determined to travel the world to verify every inch of what he was learning. Francina replied, "*Photography?* Well I guess traveling the world would be suitable for that." I paused for a moment, wondering if Francina had the strength to follow this in detail. "No Francina, *Geography*. You know, the study of the earth."

"Ohhhh," she replied and then continued, "*Geography!* This month's National Geographic has the *most* fascinating article about computerized cartography. They can do the most *wonderful* things with map making these days. Tell Tom to be sure not to miss it."

My thoughts stood corrected. At ninety-two, Francina was more current than I could ever hope to be.

The telephone call I dreaded, but also had hoped would come one day (just to be acknowledged), came January 1, 2000.

My friend Dawn answered my phone and handed it to me with a perplexed look. As I put the receiver to my ear I knew why. Hearing the beginnings of the deeply textured Georgian voice, I felt the message before the words arrived. Time lurched for a moment. And then all was fine. Francina had chosen her passing fittingly.

She was born at the dawn of the twentieth century, lived and aged more gracefully than the times themselves and then quietly slipped through as the entire world in its false bravado, stood poised to greet the uncertainty of the new millennium.

As Matthew and I stood that New Year's Eve, surrounded by laughing children and sparklers in our driveway, I felt compelled to spend a quick moment alone.

I paused in front of our house; the midnight sky bright with the moon, stars and snow all reflecting each other's glow, and felt an incredible sense of closeness surround me. The universe was tangible.

My friend was with me.

The next morning, as I listened to Nancy, Francina's cherished daughter-in-law, recount her last days I whispered a prayer of thanks for being remembered.

And then I focused more clearly as Nancy discussed the details of Francina's planned memorial. "You *know*," she lamented, "*nothing* our family does is ever easy. We have called *every* florist in the entire state of Georgia and of course there is not *one* flower left after this New Year's Eve."

We both chuckled and agreed thankfully that Francina would prefer things done simply.

My last two visits with Francina remain strong in my mind:

Delayed by airplanes and airports, I arrived later than promised both times. As I rushed into the assisted living wing during the first, I was told by the care giver at the nurses' station that Francina, after waiting patiently in the community lounge for her "friend from Wisconsin", had retired to her room for a nap.

I quietly walked into the hospital-like room recognizing instantly the one last bureau and bedside table that marked Francina's half of the room. The bed next to hers was empty and the far side of the room glowed in the warm June sun. Francina slept soundly, so I quietly reached for a book from the table next to her and went to sit in the light from the window.

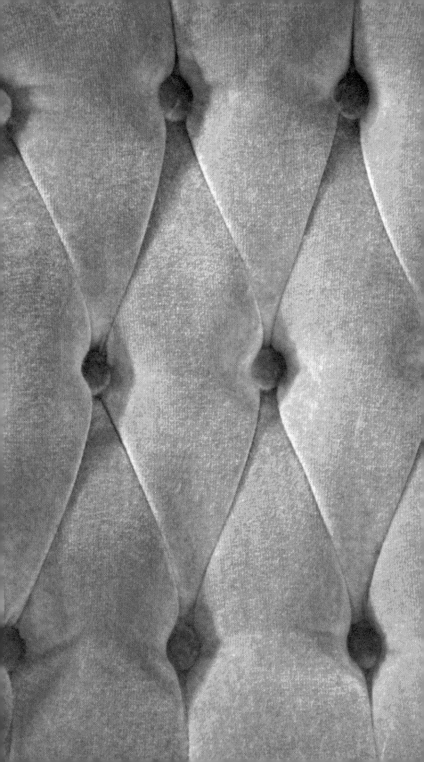

What struck me then and now was the incredible sense of peace and centeredness I felt immediately as I settled into the chair in the corner. I had left Milwaukee in a blizzard after a terrifying ride to the airport that morning, and then faced the frustration of Atlanta's Hartsfield baggage mishandlers.

Next, the traffic careening toward downtown Atlanta reminded me quickly of how small my current community is (at that point I was sure that I would never see it or my sweet children and husband again). By the time I reached Francina's bedside I was, simply put, a mess. I was questioning the sanity of ever leaving my house.

A moment later, with Francina's book in my hand and her gentle breathing by my side, everything changed. I slowly turned the first pages of the book and smiled. Francina was in the midst of a philosophical study of

God's presence in today's world and had filled almost every margin with questions, notations and reminders to herself of points to investigate further. Almost every other line was underlined or embellished with extra punctuation.

I realized that Francina treasured this book as a longtime companion and it gave me comfort just to hold it. Not long into my wait, Francina began to stir. I walked over and stood by her as she slowly regained awareness. She smiled sweetly, her blue eyes gently looking me over as I greeted her. "Hello," she replied and then continued, "are you our speaker for this evening?" I began to explain myself when she stopped me quickly and said "Oh *honey*, I am so **sorry**. Of course it's you."

And we began our visit.

I was not alone in my final visit with Francina. Jeanne joined me (this time without hair styling apparatus) and we found Francina in bed in her room with the one last standing chest of drawers loaded, of course, with family pictures and the lone, comfy occasional chair situated in the window's light.

She was in a 'light consciousness', drifting easily from sleep to wake, past to present, real to surreal. She recognized Jeanne as a friend or family member from the distant past and was pleased to see her.

Francina then entered a stage of acute lucidness, grasping our eyes with her faded blues and declared, "We have *a lot* of work to do, girls. And it's up to you two to carry the torch." We nodded solemnly, smiled, and assured Francina that we were up for the task.

I knew in that instant the amount of pure goodness contained in her room was irreplaceable and the world was about to lose a seismic amount of positive energy that would truly be our loss.

Peace

And are we up for carrying the torch? As the world progresses past the millennium growing pains, the horrors of the Twin Towers (which we of course will always grieve) and a bully child masked as leader of the one, lone supposed superpower, I wonder where Francina would stand among the fray.

I know her mantra was faith. I hear her voice, see the light in her eyes and feel her determination that we are ultimately good and try to greet each precious moment first with a smile.

Life before Francina, life after Francina. Has any one touched me more? Very few as much, or as gently, so profoundly.

Francina's Letters to Anne

Anne, dear friend-

You and Matthew and Robby have been in
my thoughts since you were here Thursday
night. I was with you all the way and do
hope it was an easy trip-and now you are
there, *home*, and I am envisioning all the
things you're doing. Thank you dear heart
for the lovely roses and for being my
friend. I love you. Love to Matthew.
God Bless.

Fondly,
Francina

Anne dear,

I loved your telephone call. You sounded so upbeat and happy, and that makes me happy. I *wish* I could see your garden! Atlanta is a dream of white and pink dogwood, pansies and various other blooming trees. We had a lovely Easter. This little card was drawn by the principal cellist in the Atlanta Symphony Orchestra. My niece and I go regularly. So many other things are going on. I can't recount. I love you and *miss* you. If you do come to Atlanta I'm looking forward to you staying with me. Love to all the family.

Devotedly,
Francina

Dear Anne,

Loved your card-I think of you and
Matthew and Robby-experiencing with you,
pleasurably, your new lovely home, excited
about your plans for it, anticipating your
garden, the fun of the winter snow and
the skiing. I'm so *sorry* Robby has an ear
infection and hoping it will subside soon.
I can hardly realize that little boy is
two years old. I remember so warmly my joy
in your having him. I'm so glad to hear he
likes Beloit.

Spring is beginning to show her face. The
pear trees are about to burst into bloom.
The pansies and jonquil are gorgeous. The
March weather is being itself-erratic. I
think it's great you're planning to start
writing; I need to do that too, but the
children want me to talk on tape telling
some stories my mother told me-family
stuff. I'm not good at that. I can do it
better in writing.

You and Matthew will be in my prayers
regarding the business opportunities.
Don't worry-remember this is an adventure.
I believe all will be well. I'm sorry to
miss your call. I love you, dear friend.

Fondly,
Francina

Anne dear,

I'm back home and plan to *stay* awhile. In early June I took the family to the beach. Then on the 18th went to Arizona for a family reunion and that was special. We took two or three days after that and did a little sight seeing. Visited the Grand Canyon, staying at the old El Tovar Hotel and then on to Sedona…fascinating place. Now just back from attending a conference at Asbury College and it was really good. So now I have my place on the market and am making plans to move, don't know just when. How is little Robby? I know he is happy to have his Mama around so much more than in Atlanta. Give Matthew my love and heaps and heaps for your own self. I miss you.

Much love,
Francina

Anne dear-

Loved your note and really loved our
little visit. You always do me good. And
its fun to think of you in your lovely
home and beautiful garden. We have really
been working, getting packed up to move
on the 24th. I still have much to do-
with boxes labeled 'Bobbie Lee' (maid
upstairs), 'Orphan Home' and 'Church
Clothes Closet'.

I thought I had narrowed down when I came
here but I really am doing it now. I
have only a one bedroom apartment but I
bought a brand new sofa bed which is in
the living room. Remember that I *count* on
having you with me when next you come.
Much love always.

Devotedly,
Francina

Anne dear,

You have been so much in my thoughts and
it did me a lot of good to hear your
lovely, crisp voice the other day on the
phone and I am so happy you are coming to
Atlanta. I just wish our plans could fit a
bit better, but it will be great to have a
glimpse of you and Jeanne on the 11th of
June.

Atlanta is perfectly beautiful with the
dogwood., azalea, and pansies in profusion.
I'm wondering how far along your garden is
at this point. I am on the flower committee
at Canterbury Court with a partner. I'm in
charge of doing the flowers for the month
of April. I am looking forward to seeing
you on the 11th.

Much love,
Francina

Anne dear,

I loved hearing your voice the other day.
It was sweet of you to call. I'm still
trying to get *organized* but beginning to
feel at home. This place is a community
within itself. I'm involved in the Stephen
Ministry - an effort to be a friend to
someone in some sort of crisis...do
this with the guidance of the Pavilion
(infirmary) administrator. There's much
more to it than just that. We had a pipe
break recently and *flooded* the ground floor;
all the floor covering is ruined. It's been
good to chat with you. *I love you.*

Fondly,
Francina

Anne dear,

It was so good to hear your voice the other day and I am so happy for you and Matthew in the advent of your second little son. Benjamin and Robby will be such pals. I had been thinking of you constantly not sure when the baby was due. Before long your lovely garden is going to burst into bloom and you will enjoy it so much. I hope one of these days to see it. I truly hope that you are now feeling well and that the baby is fine. I think I am getting over the trauma of this move. Adjusting has taken longer than I thought it would. I will hope you can come in late Spring. We must not lose touch. I miss you! *You are Special.*

Much love to you.
Francina

Anne dear,

I have been thinking of you and hoping
all is settled in regards to that awful
experience you had. I do hope that
you are completely over the trauma. Do let
me know that all is well. Your are in my
thoughts, and my prayers and *I love you*.

Devotedly,
Francina

Anne dear,

I loved our visit, only it was too short.
The Hotel Nikko tea was *special*, thank you
so much. You look wonderful. I hate for
you to be so far away but it does look
like a good move for you. I do hope the
new business venture is working out *fine*
and we must remember that a venture of
this size takes a while to build. I wish
I could see your two boys. I know you are
enjoying them-children are so fascinating
to watch in their development. Tomorrow
I'm going on a bus trip, visiting the
different places being developed for the
Olympic Games. I'll write you about what I
see. Much love and come back soon.

Fondly,
Francina

Anne darling,

Thank you for your dear note. It was such a joy to see you and little Benjamin. You looked wonderful, no reflection of what you have been through. I'll be thinking of you and lifting a prayer that what you have to do will be done as quickly and as smoothly as possible to accomplish its purpose. We had a cute 4th of July picnic here at Canterbury with much decoration, etc. I decided to stay here instead of getting with my 'chillun'. I want to develop friendships here. Thank you for your dear invitation to visit you and I would *love* that. There may be a time when it would work out. *Much* love to you dear, and Matthew and the boys.

Fondly,
Francina

Anne dear,

I've been thinking about you and the boys and want to touch base with you. I miss you. Lots have been going on with us. I am beginning to feel at home at Canterbury Court, making friends. I recently sold my car which is traumatic. The last little bit of independence gone! But I'm sure it's the right thing to do. A lovely young woman (lives up the street) picks me up for our 'Stephen Ministry' meetings every other week. And our little van makes regular trips to mall, etc. Now I've run out of paper…I just wanted to say Hi and send my love.

Fondly,
Francina

Anne dear,

If I had written as often as I've thought
of you, you would be *showered* with mail.
I am still trying to get back on my feet
and feeling better. I am going to meals
and doing usual things but *resting* a lot.
I think I over-did it at one point. The
only excitement around here was the alarm
system going off at 2 a.m. the other
night. I got up and looked around but no
one was stirring so went back to bed. It
was funny…they didn't announce it was a
false alarm but I guess everyone just
figured it was. The voice on the alarm was
different than the one we practiced with.

I hope you had a grand summer. After
dinner tonight three of us sat in the big
rockers overlooking the garden and it was
so pleasant.

Much love to you, Matthew and the boys.
Francina

Anne dear heart,

What can I say? *How* can I respond to your beautiful 'memory piece.' I have just come from lunch, stopped to pick up the mail and just *now* finished reading your notes. I'm still wiping the tears. There is no *way* to respond. It will remain a treasure to me for always, tho' I feel so unworthy of the beautiful things that you said. I have to tell you tho', that I rejoice to hear you say that you found some help for your own Faith Journey from me. I have asked the Lord to send His Love through me, and what you say makes me feel that maybe He *is* doing that. I have not started my piece on our friendship but will *soon*. However I send this on so you will know I'm really going to do it. You are so special to me and you have helped *me* so much.

Devotedly,
Francina

Excerpts from Francina's Rough Draft

"…when I resumed speed, a car was coming which the trees obscured, so I ran into the side of this car. For awhile I was in shock, then I realized a car was stopped and a lovely person was coming over to offer help. My thoughts…what a lovely young woman and how beautifully she is dressed! Immediately I accepted her offer gratefully and gave her some telephone numbers to call…"

"The next day a lovely vase of flowers come to me from Anne. And I discovered that she was grieving for a baby she had recently lost. Bless her, how could she do that for someone unknown to her. Dare I think that the effort to help someone else made it possible to be at ease about her own grief?"

"After my stay in the hospital my thoughts turned to how I could do something for Anne. I decided on a whole beef tenderloin and asked Anne to come pick it up.

And that's how Anne and I began our friendship. I asked
her over and she came and we discovered that we liked each
other and shared several interests. So we began having a little
sandwich lunch and grew to be fast friends.

Then, Anne became pregnant again and I prayed for her and
the new baby and rejoiced when the little boy was delivered…
a perfect baby."

"Now we have been separated as Anne and family have
moved to Wisconsin where they used to live. I think they
did the right thing. I miss her so much…her warmth, and
friendship and her growing awareness of spiritual matters…

More to be added"

E-mail from Francina's daughter-in-law,
Nancy, post Francina's memorial service

.

Anne,

I can't tell you what an impact your story of your relationship with Francina made on everyone that read it. In fact, we made several copies to hand out to people who asked for it and Clarke, our son, who did the eulogy, referred to it. He particularly read the part about "enjoying life based on faith as opposed to fear". Thank you so much for sharing it.

Monday, the day of the graveside service, started out in light rain and fog. However, by the time we got to West Point, GA, the sun was shining and it was between 65 and 70 degrees! I wonder when the last time January 3rd can boast of that weather? There was a steady breeze as we sat under the two tents, listened to and gave our own remembrances of Francina. Several of the grandchildren read the scriptures and then we sang the Lord's Prayer and a song that we sing as a family every Thanksgiving, "Give Thanks." It was a wonderful service and her body is now lying next to Wib and near her own parents. You were a precious friend to her and she loved you very much.

Affectionately,
Nancy

*A friend sent me this as a condolence upon
hearing of Francina's passing.*

Gone From My Sight

(Henry Van Dyke, 1852-1933)

"I am standing upon the seashore. A ship at my side spreads her white sails in the morning breeze and starts for the blue ocean. She is an object of beauty and strength and I stand and watch her until at length she is only a ribbon of white cloud just where the sea and sky come to mingle with each other. Then, someone at my side says, 'There! She's gone!'

"Gone where? Gone from my sight–that is all. She is just as large in mast and hull and spar as she was when she left my side, and just as able to bear her load of living freight to the place of destination. Her diminished size is in me, not her, and just at the moment when someone at my side says, 'There, she is gone!' there are other voices ready to take up the glad shout, 'Here she comes!'

And that is dying."

Postscript

It has been over ten years since I began this journey of sharing my thoughts on my friendship with Francina and several years since her passing. I miss her dearly. In reviewing this work in its entirety I realized I left a few 'hanging chads' but did not want to distract from the main focus of my writing which was solely about the course of our friendship. So here are some updates:

Our son, Tom, recovered from his coma and head injury against extreme odds. Never supposedly to walk or talk again, he amazed everyone with his fierce determination and ended up graduating with his high school class, played soccer again, pursued a degree in geography from the University of Wisconsin, fell in love, got married and is now raising his very busy three year-old son. His passion is writing and hopefully after the pre-school years, we will be graced with his special ability to share his voice.

After four long years of pursuit, the very sick doctor who delivered my son Ben finally had his medical license stripped from all the states he worked in as a traveling fill-in physician and was forced into an early retirement. It gives me great relief to know he will not be able to harm another woman during childbirth and physical examinations. He left a wide path of destruction and needed to be stopped. The upside is that my son Ben made it through the delivery unscathed and now is truly a very special force in our universe.

Acknowledgements

I ran across a quote a long time ago by Luciano De Creschenzo: "We are each of us angels with only one wing. And we can only fly embracing each other." The working title of this essay was "When Angels Meet." Francina and I certainly achieved angel status in each other's lives. And what I've learned along the way is we're constantly offered opportunities to be angels to one another. My heartfelt thanks and appreciation to the many angels who supported the effort to bring my story to 'little book' status, especially Miki Herman for her steadfast belief that this "will be a book", Jeanne Holbrook for 'getting it' and sharing Francina with me, Becky Moffett for her helpful insight and steady encouragement, Jeff Larson and Judy Knowler of the Larson Group for 'seeing it' and to Matthew Goodwin for 'being it' always for me.